Immigrant Prodigal Daughter

Immigrant Prodigal Daughter

Poems by

Lucia Cherciu

Cover design by Shay Culligan
Cover image by Vasile Diaconu
Author's photo by Karl Barth

ISBN: 978-1-63980-341-5

Kelsay Books
502 South 1040 East, A-119
American Fork, Utah 84003
Kelsaybooks.com

Acknowledgments

Many thanks to the editors of the publications in which some of these poems appeared previously.

Albany Poets: "Language and Maps," "The Chronic Confidence of Want," "The Romanian Blouse"
Bookends Review: "Return"
Briar Cliff Review: "Tango on the Boulevards in the City"
Cape Rock Review: "Organic Flowers from My Garden"
Chiron Review: "Cutting the Grass with a Scythe," Bequeathed to Me"
Citron Review: "Immigrant Verbs"
Comstock Review: "All That Light"
Cortland Review: "November after Elections," "Rituals"
Edison Literary Review: "They Knit the Truth"
Innisfree Poetry Journal: "The Apple Trees from Home," "The Season of Giving"
Lightwood: "Fighting the Urge to Clean"
Masque and Spectacle: "Prostrations"
Miracle Monocle: "What Advice Would Mircea Dinutz, My Teacher of Latin, Give Me?"
Newtown Review: "Scarce Temptations," "Everyday Rituals"
Paterson Literary Review: "Ars Poetica"
Poetry East: "We Didn't Listen"
Sidereal: "The Privilege of Water"
Sleet: "Socially Distanced June," "Prayer for an Apricot Tree," "My Sister and I Bought the First Books in Our House," "The Miracle of Dawn"
Stone Canoe: "I Thought We Had More Time"
Voices on the Move Anthology: "Blue Wrapping Paper," "Haircuts in the Backyard," "Prayer for an Apricot Tree"

Special Thanks

For all my generous teachers, including Cristina Mazilu, Mircea Dinutz, Gheorghe Zaharia, Monica Pillat, Ioana Zirra, Ioana Gogeanu, and Karen Dandurand. With gratitude, to John R. Peters-Campbell, whose lessons about art inspire and energize. To my writing friends, who are supportive and kind: Jan Zlotnik Schmidt, Judith Saunders, and Raphael Kosek.

Always, for Betty and Murray Ross, Deanna Speer, and David Naylor.

For my parents, Ioana and Ion.

With love, for Madeline and Karl.

Contents

III

I

Immigrant Prodigal Daughter

After Rembrandt, "The Return of the Prodigal Son"

Immigrants carry the burden of sin:
they left behind their fathers

who waited for them all their lives.
Every day, parents looked towards the gate

hoping beyond miracle. Every night, mothers
prayed. The courage it takes to uproot

for a new country, a new language, leaving
friends of a lifetime, path to the house.

Immigrants wrangle unwieldy
hopes. In their ears, a mother's wails.

The witness who knows and understands
stands in the middle, aware, astute:

a mirror, envisioning the truth.
A witness often withholds

the relevant detail. In the shade, the prodigal
daughter: what is left of love, what spills over,

the ignored, the remainder. The munificence
and wisdom it takes to welcome them back

as they are, triumphant or forlorn. The old world
dispenses with them, learns to go on without.

Hungry to fold them in, the new world uses them,
judges them, or refuses to invite them at the table.

Tango on the Boulevards in the City

I dance with your laughter:
the city opens its arms, lights on,

bookstores galore, chocolate voluptuous.
Boulevards tempting, galleries lush with secrets:

everything you have touched has blossomed,
everything you have wished for has arrived,

everything purple and blue has tuliped.
Stilettoes and turquoise, fishnet stockings

and watercolors, stealthiness and persistence:
the sound of your steps on the marble of the plaza.

Osmosis. Singlemindedness. Willfulness.
Obstinacy dredges up insomnia and doubt:

everything you have painted
has brought about a tango of innuendo:

you have hypnotized the moon—
you have cheated on me with me.

The Apple Trees from Home

I didn't know I already had everything.
Abundance and fear. Abundance of fear.

I defied darkness. I had my health.
I prayed to remember. I prayed to forget.

I followed the light, sought the light in others.
Tried to name the four kinds of pears

grafted on my grandparents' pear tree.
Dreamed all night I was picking

summer apples, cherries, plums
from all our fruit trees I left behind. Why

did you leave, asks my mother.
Don't worry, time will pass

and soon you'll come home again,
my father used to say. I didn't

tell them I wanted to stay.
I should have called more often.

I followed the routine. Feigned a routine.
I fasted. I ate my restlessness.

I pined for a white porch that evaded me.
I longed for a hundred kinds of grapes.

I listened to the lingering litany of birds
I couldn't name and I laughed.

Grammar Is a Map

Grammar is a map: the words I know in another language
are like benches in the shade where a friend

waits for me in every town and holds my hand.
My tour guide for an ancient city, each sentence

has wisdom to impart: stand tall. Send money
to your sister. Write a note with seven reasons

you respect your brother. Grammar is a map:
what a miracle to be here. What a heavenly gift

to breathe in this thought with these words
that I was not born into. How I miss the milk

of my mother's songs. Delicate or rustic,
the words in my native tongue remind me

of a gate, a porch, and a threshold:
o poartă, un pridvor, şi un prag. Grammar

is a bride of promises, a lattice of veils.
Grammar is a groom of confidence:

imparts strength and secrets, teaches
with tenderness. To speak in another language

is to be courageous and humble, to ask
for forgiveness with each syllable, each gesture.

Please forgive my offenses, forget my mistakes
because I have learned every word

in another language with prayer and sweat.
I have walked the country of your grammar,

listened and repeated, and have yet to learn
to let go of my trespasses. All the words

in other languages I have grasped
have taught me the sweetness of silence—

if I had kept quiet, I'd still be a philosopher:
Dacă tăceai, filosof rămâneai.

This Summer I Cannot Travel Home

Kindness and apricots. The kindness of apricots.
A window bench with pillows, books,

and tapestries from home. I haven't been to Romania
in four years. And this summer again we're not going

home. Not going home is like not drinking coffee:
I am half asleep, half dreaming, half lost.

Why have I left? Was my mother not enough?
Were my books not enough? Were my friends

not enough? Not going home is like living in a house
with small windows and a low ceiling: I cannot walk tall.

In the kitchen, a nook that looks like a booth
in an old coffee house. Reading

with a cup of ginger tea: my mother is sitting
on both sides of the table. She looks like me.

She has let her hair go gray. Mother,
I am not traveling home this summer. Tomorrow

I will buy another hundred books. Tomorrow
I will plant more fruit trees. Tomorrow

I will ask any friends I might have wronged
to forgive me. It's my fault that this summer

I am not returning home. It's not my fault
that this summer I'm not arriving home.

Waiting for the apricot blossoms to take,
watching the fruit form, I am always already home.

The Season of Giving

Don't buy me anything. Send me a picture
of small treasures in your house: a copy

of a sepia portrait of your grandmother,
an old blue scarf you haven't worn in twenty years,

some earrings you received as a gift in high school
and never wore. Ask me to choose.

I have to want it first. Then I will take
five pictures of treasures from my house:

a Romanian ceramic plate, an embroidered
shawl from North Transylvania.

You choose one. Objects we already have
in the house, sealed in boxes in the basement

because of chronic allergies to dust.
We can give the bits of money we save

to a poor family to pay their heating bill.
With the bits of money we save, we can buy

some time to learn a new prayer by heart.
How many prayers do you know by heart?

How many languages do you pray in?
In what language does God speak to you?

This season, I will write a prayer
for my benefactors, who have brought me here,

who have watched me on my journey
farther and farther from home.

Cutting Grass with a Scythe

I imagine my father lies down on the bed,
propping his head on two pillows and says,

"Come and sit here next to me."
The first year after revolution he lost his job.

He is fifty-two. He will never have
a full-time job again, but he doesn't know that

yet. Two of us have started college in Bucharest,
my brother is going away to military school at fourteen,

and my father will never make a full-time salary
again. He will sell carnations at the farmer's market;

he will work for a friend and sell vegetables for him.
He will work as a daily laborer in summer.

He will pack and unload sacks of flour
at the bread factory where my mother works

and he will catch his asthma there
with coughing spells that will last ten minutes straight.

But he doesn't know all that yet.
He asks me to sit down next to him

as he tells me stories about people
I have never met. Something that happened

in his youth. He laughs. In summer,
he works a daily job cutting grass

with a scythe in the field. He sings
although his hands bubble and bleed.

Bequeathed to Me

We work too hard,
don't obsess about hair
don't do our nails.
We buy cheap shoes that hurt
so we have to buy another pair
and that one is even cheaper
because we feel guilty that we bought a new one.

We buy cheap clothes
and then we don't like them because they look cheap.
We don't have enough room to organize our cheap clothes
and end up wearing the same ten pieces
because we cannot find the other ones
and all of them look cheap anyway.

We love our family with food,
heal ourselves with food
show love with food,
express our faith with food
deny ourselves food
make public our restraint from food
plan our weeks around food
consider ourselves worthy
because we control our food.

We communicate with our dead with food
send them food
make them their favorite *plăcinte*
bake for them round whole-wheat bread
spend a whole day wrapping *sarmale*
and give it all to an old man who can't cook.

Somewhere, our fathers wish
we had better sat down
and rested against the back of the chair,
breathed. Maybe they wish
we had prepared less food.

I Thought We Had More Time

I thought we had more time—summer and apricots—
stalling, backpedaling, prevaricating.

Umbrellas and intimacy—a basket of fruit
left on the porch when we're in love.

My old car and the smell of golden delicious.
Almonds and alms, raspberries and reasons.

Bicycles and prayer: only those who believe
dare this narrow road with repentance.

I scraped my knees, tried to remember
the ascetic, the lapidary, the levitating power

of words learned by heart. Has anyone told you
that the upwelling of joy in your voice

has done more than ten thousand books,
a hundred rivers, an orchard full of forgiveness?

Ars Poetica

During lent, when I was fourteen,
women made stuffed cabbage
for *pomană,* the meal for the village,
while the body rested in the good room.

Old people stayed with her
to make sure the candle didn't go out.
She was never by herself. All night long,
uninvited, people came to the wake.

During the day, women sang dirges—
improvised poems that rhymed:
"Why did you go, Tudură, and left me alone?
Your three boys, now three men,

don't have a mother anymore."
I watched how they composed their songs.
A woman sang a line
and then broke into crying.

She wove in bits from the life
of the departed, details
that could bring back the dead.
A month before, my grandmother had asked me,

"When I die, will you sing dirges for me?"
She had three sons and doubted
her daughters-in-law would sing for her.
Women started to sing a dirge

when more people came in the house:
"Tudură, Tudură, why have you left me?"
The singer stood by the head
and touched the hands, fixed something

that went awry, smoothed the hair
on the pillow.
I waited until everyone came in
and I spoke my dirges. I didn't sing them

and didn't rhyme
because there was too much going on.
On the way back from the cemetery,
walking up the hill, one of her sisters

gave me a piece of hard candy
and told me to remember that day.
My mother carried back the pillow
on which the head had rested.

It had some hand-embroidered flowers
with blue and green thread
and for years I slept on it
when we went back to the old house.

On the face of the pillow
the fabric was folded in ripples
sewn by my grandmother
on her sewing machine.

We Bought the First Books in Our House

What if our destiny was decided by how many books
we had in our house when we started to read?

When I was twelve and my sister fourteen, we each
bought the same book: *Barefoot* by Zaharia Stancu,

which cost twenty *lei*. With that money each of us
could have bought ten bags of *caramele*

or eight eclairs, but we wanted to own
our own books. When we went away to college

neither of us took those books. Now my mom
could read *Barefoot* by Zaharia Stancu

to her heart's content: she could underline in one
and keep the other copy clean. Well, nobody

read *Barefoot* because it turned out the author
sold out to communists, even though

that novel was not half bad. I remember
the episode in the wheat field

where a woman gave birth to twins
and her mother-in-law cut the umbilical cord with a scythe

in the scorching July heat. Growing up,
we bought the first books in our house,

spent more money on books than on dresses.
Maybe I should have bought new sandals

instead of some of those stilted,
stultifying communist books.

Propagating Rosemary Is a Form of Faith

Propagating rosemary is a form of faith—
rooting softwood cuttings of lavender,

herbs I have planted myself, used them for tea
and shared them with friends.

Welcome plants and compassion. A cup
of rosemary tea on an early afternoon

when guests cannot come over to sit
under the maple tree. Giving away calendula for tea,

plants that are still alive, that I have transplanted
myself, whether I took cuttings or, miraculously,

I grew them from seeds. Have you grown basil
from seeds? Or even, worthier of respect,

have you grown chamomile from seeds?
Suffused with peace. Frail, the tendrils of plants—

like the balance of uttering just enough words. Fierce,
they resist the frost. Welcome lemon balm,

lemon verbena, so your friends can transplant them
in their garden or place them on the windowsill

in their kitchen. This morning, while I start
a new rosemary plant, I invoke the faith

to revise. Inspiration. Enthusiasm.
I give words of praise. Wild thyme.

Reclaim spring. Reinvent optimism
and hope. Listen in. Open the door.

Old Clocks and Nasturtiums

I gave up wearing a watch about ten years ago. Watches
in the house: perennial lilies that return faithfully

of their own accord. Like a friend who wears a mask
and sits outside under the maple tree on the spaced chairs.

My grandfather had an old clock that played a song.
I remember seeing the inside of that clock as he tried

to repair it. This spring the clematis did not return.
The cosmos seeds I planted did not germinate. How many

clocks do you own? Do you remember the clocks
you used to have in the house when you were a child?

Do you remember the zinnias your grandmother planted?
Every time somebody fixed an old clock was a miracle.

Every time somebody grew echinacea from seed
was a miracle. Every time somebody drove to my house

with an echinacea plant from their garden was a miracle.
Today it is my turn to start basil from seeds. To leave out

plants on my neighbors' porches. To comfort others
with daisies started from seeds. To ignore the clocks,

dispose of broken things beyond repair.
Hindsight praises the stoics who stood by their friends

despite mistakes. Undeniably, nasturtiums
become a way of fixing old clocks, honoring the memory

of a face that looked up in wonder, with surprise
of recognition. If you only knew how much I praised you!

How Many Hours Have I Spent Revising My Novel?

I'm doing this one-thousand-piece puzzle.
It's like these kittens are making mischief.

I've done the edges. I'm not very far along.
My daughter is talking to her teacher online. After

her ninety-minute class, the child reaches out to me,
bluish with exhaustion, leans into a hug

and asks me to help her with her puzzle.
Unlike my daughter, I don't like puzzles

with more than twenty-four pieces.
Revising my novel took a hundred times longer

than writing the first draft. *It's like the words*
are making mischief. How many hours

have I spent revising my novel? Instead,
I should have taken my daughter out for a walk

to get our daily vitamin D. The novel
might fracture with so much revision.

I have taken out what was risky and brave.
My bones are brittle with so much revision.

The Immigrant Mother's Lament

When you visit a house with small children,
bring a riddle, a story, a picture of a bird.

Something not made of plastic,
not baked with sugar.

Bring a prayer book. Help parents
break the spell of screens

through the effortless devotion of verbs.
Show them how to teach

the rhyme of contentment,
echo words in the native language,

give praise. I have taken my child
away from my mother.

I have reneged on my promises.
I have become a bridge. I have recognized my mother

in my child's face. Traced the steps.
And all the longing that lured me away.

We Didn't Listen

Growing up we read all these novels, but sometimes
we didn't think of what they were really about.

We read *Ion,* but we didn't talk about rape.
We read *Şatra,* but we didn't mention the holocaust.

Sometimes we sang along songs, but we didn't
listen to the lyrics. There was one song

about gang rape, but we didn't pay attention
to what it said, and sang along

because the beat was good and the teachers
didn't stop us either. The lyrics cut pathways

into our brains: "They take the girl to their home
on the street with two linden trees

and because she is beautiful,
they fight among themselves."

What do songs do when we are not listening?
Do songs build their own roads, their own back alleys?

At Night in a Second Language

The ritual of waking up at night, the endowment:
the house reverberates with quiet mantras.

Outside, an owl calls, deer nibble on dahlias,
munch on red peppers, spare the mums.

Inside, dreams are spinning a second moonlight
intersecting between rooms. In one dream

pronouns lead the parade. In another, predicates
make the windows spin. Sentences long as the clouds

unfurling. Awake when everybody sleeps:
a world that gives itself, denies itself,

insults itself by wasting time. At midnight here,
it's 7 AM back home, and my mother gets ready

to head to the market to buy carrots for soup.
In my mother tongue, dream and reality are one,

words and the substance they are made of are one,
nouns and the entities they name are one,

and mysteries birth verbs, verbs, verbs.

Traveling to Another Country

Sleep is all about the light. If one could project
on a screen what we see when we dream—

a film laced with lists of images, a loom.
Somebody weaves the lines of loss.

The threads of memory hold tight
the summer of return: the triumphant

smile of those who keep their hope,
who persist in their quests despite

others' doubts and denials. Sleep
is the ultimate form of trust and faith:

being with you means knowing your arms
are always around me, even in despair.

Making a promise is like finding a path
in the dark: the steps familiar, comforting,

despite threats. The glow of the moon.
Towards dawn, the enchanting honor

of traveling back, order reinstated,
equilibrium restored. Arrival home.

My Daughter Doesn't Want to Go Home

When she was two, traveling to Romania was easy:
I picked her up and carried her in my arms around the world.

Our flight over the ocean, a blissful snuggle. Cradled
in the soft swing of the plane, after the piercing excitement

of the take off. As she started to grow, it became harder
to convince her. The last time we went, she cried

all the way through the security line at Newark airport.
The flight itself was easy, between movies, packed snacks,

and flight attendants who spoiled us. When we got to the customs,
I had to coax her to get close to officers, as if she knew

that people who entered forgot all hope of escape. In Romania,
everyone gave her gifts. My mom bought a white bunny

just weaned off and we let him hop around in the house.
The whole month, a whirl of fluffy soft fur. My daughter

smothered him. The whole month, her Romanian language
came back. My mother, the only one who doesn't speak English,

became an archetypal well of words. By then, my daughter
sang whole songs, recounted stories, told jokes in Romanian.

Last year, my daughter didn't want to go home,
though my mother promised her a bunny, a duckling, and a dog.

This year is Covid and we cannot travel. I have tried
praying and playing, fairy tales and lullabies, so when we go home

my daughter can speak to my mother, weave words together.
"It's not my home," my daughter tells me; "it's your home."

II

Look at My Father

The earrings you gave me twenty-six years ago
remind me that I am not allowed to waste time

because I am my father's daughter. I carry a burden
because I have left home and moved to another country.

I can't be lazy because I am my mother's daughter
and she never rests. I am lazy because hard work

did not bring her any rewards. When I was four,
a Roma walked down on our road in the mountains,

carrying dozens of earrings. I was sitting on the stone
in front of our gate and he asked me which pair of earrings

I wanted. I chose small drops of metal. He pierced
my ears right there in front of our gate. It didn't hurt.

How those earrings glittered! My father laughed
and paid the man. We chased my sister all the way

up the hill in the back of our garden so she
could get her ears pierced, but she didn't stay.

I want to look the way my father looked at me.
I look like my father, now gone for nineteen years.

I change my earrings so they can catch your eye
when you look at me, so you can see my father.

All That Light

The painting you gave me reminds me of hell—
and that's not a bad thing—reminds me to not set

any price. We planted fruit trees and perennials,
but sold the house. When we arrived,

we found peonies, lilacs. Summer opened up
to its deceits. Self-justifying, fall collected

all the receipts. Only in winter did we really fathom
the depth of our debt: who brewed for us

a fresh cup of tea, who gave us bread
when we were broke. Who broke us

or gave us a break. The painting you gave me
reminds me of hell: I made mistakes.

I tried too hard. I didn't try enough. Books
I didn't finish. Money I didn't give away.

I made stiff pronouncements—
that unfortunately turned out

to be right. Wasted exuberance—
I wasted all that light. Tonight,

I sit by your painting and raise a glass
to everything promised, to everything denied.

Spring Is a Reminder of Paradise

For Vasile Diaconu (1954–2021)

When I take off my glasses it's all a blur: the framed picture
recedes the way the airplane takes off when we leave.

My uncle sent me a picture he took—a talented photographer
before everyone used smart phones, when pictures were rare.

A haystack enclosed by a fence in the center of a meadow
so wild animals don't get to it in the middle of winter.

Surrounded by cowslip flowers, *primula officinalis,*
the landscape is the purest image of home.

The yellow flowers hold the kindness of regret.
Garden forsaken. The person who gathered that hay didn't

return to feed the animals. A truce with time,
the flowers pledge that this year will be better. We'll celebrate

spring with rituals and ceremonies. Innocence.
Laughter, stories, dance, generosity. Maybe loneliness.

Maybe the way he collected so many broken TVs and gadgets
in need of repair is like the drafts left unrevised,

projects left unfinished, invitations not honored,
questions left unanswered, questions I didn't ask.

Revising a draft is like returning home every summer—one year
we are together sitting around the table under the willow tree

and the next year we face the empty side of the table,
the echo of surprises, the silence of promises.

Blue Wrapping Paper

Wrapping a box in shiny blue paper, I remember the surprise.
When I had nothing, I knew how to appreciate everything.

Somebody had cut a branch off the fir-tree and brought it inside.
That Christmas my uncle brought me candy and chocolate

wrapped in royal blue paper. I try to remember
what kind of chocolate it was. The gifts over the years.

This March, he returned to his house late, too sick to make a fire.
The ambulance came, carried him to three different hospitals

that wouldn't take him. Then the tests confirmed he had Covid.
Finally, one hospital kept him. The family was not allowed to visit.

His discharged phone. We stayed up late praying, tethered to hope.
My mother kept the lights on all night, called us and cried.

On the wall, the picture he gave me some twenty years ago.
His photographs bring back places forsaken, dreams renounced.

I wrap an empty box in shiny blue paper, fold the edges back,
smooth them out, try to remember what kind of chocolate it was,

what kind of candy. I try to remember the last day I saw him,
three years ago. Have I praised him enough? Have I told him

how his gifts brightened our childhood? His countless forms
of generosity. In order to remember hope, I look at the picture

of wild hawthorns that he gave me. Sometimes
I make a list of all the gifts he brought over the years. Sometimes

in a store, some shiny blue wrapping paper arrests me
and I remember the child's anticipation of joy.

The Things Immigrants Leave Behind

It comforts me to think that although I have left
I tried to return whenever I could.

Did I know then how much I would leave behind?
Disposing of words, giving up syllables.

The guitar that my father bought for me
when I was twelve. All the books I had bought

before I turned twenty-two. Looking back
I wonder why I bought all those books to keep

even when I knew I was leaving. We are always
leaving. We always know we are leaving and yet

we cannot stop buying all those books. And yet we leave.
Unencumbered. Calm. Far away, on a sunny balcony,

my mother sits alone and checks on her geraniums,
moves the cactus away from too much sun,

takes in the beauty of the chestnut tree blossoms
in all their splendor, breathes in the aroma

of all the flowering trees in the park, listens to the bells
of the several churches within sight and waits for us to call.

What Advice Would Mircea Dinutz, My Teacher of Latin, Give Me?

I imagine him walking fast on Strada Gării, hurrying up
to our high school. At forty, his hair already white.

The collar of his threadbare coat raised up, as he tries to fight
the frost that cuts through his knuckles. He's carrying

a battered leather satchel full of papers from three high schools
from the far ends of town. He is an adjunct.

He scans the Latin verses on the blackboard. We don't
listen. Don't see him. Don't appreciate him. We are young

and foolish. He fails because he tries too hard. Maybe he
succeeds but we don't know. All the sustaining pauses

from the wooden tongue of communism.
All the sustainable distractions from having to learn

Party nonsense by heart. He sweats and frets
as he writes the declensions on the board. He is teaching us

the prologue to the *Aeneid*. We don't listen. He is a fussbudget
when it comes to teaching grammar. Though we don't listen,

we hear what he says—thirty years later. How many students
from my high school class became members of *Securitate,*

the communist secret police? One classmate planned
to become a priest but, instead, became a member of *Securitate.*

Another classmate went to the Seminary to become a priest—
and became a priest. Standing in front of all of us,

our teacher of Latin taught us, a philology class,
that the Dacians survived the Roman invasion through grammar.

Those women must have loved Latin. Those Roman
soldiers must have been good teachers of grammar.

We Only Get to Keep What We Give Away

At eighty-two, my friend is cleaning her house:
she mailed back to me the books I sent to her along the years.

What if one day we only get to keep what we gave away?
What if charisma is dangerous because one sends others

on the wrong path? Unbidden, memories return:
watching a man who is ice fishing on the lake

while we sit at the window in front of the fireplace:
she is knitting and I am studying for a French exam.

We go for a walk and practice our German. We met
at German conversation hour when I thought

I was going back to Romania at the end
of that academic year. Besieged by fear. Worry.

Diffidence. I belabor many phrases in languages
I don't speak well, but I revel in their poetry: to read

a poem by Rilke in a bilingual edition. To savor
a verse by Baudelaire. To search for poems

by Lorca and remember reading out loud his poems
in Spanish with my sister, laughing at the superb cadence

of his music. At eighty-two, my friend is cleaning her house.
All her life she has prepared to give away by giving away.

What Advice Would My Father Give Me?

To not cry after him. *Să nu-l bocesc* because I am him.
I walk his walk. I laugh his laugh. To make friends

with strangers on the bus. To remember to learn
their names. To buy for myself a nice fedora.

To go for a walk. To call my mother every other day
and listen as she regals me with stories. To make her laugh.

To write stories that make people laugh. Give something back.
Nobody wants to cry in front of their children. Remember when

he used to turn without saying goodbye because he didn't
want me to see him cry, he didn't want to make me cry?

To not look at old photographs. To call my brother
and look at him. To call my sister and look at her. To give gifts

to my nephew and nieces: what they want, not what I want.
Not what I think they want. To sit down on the steps

of our threshold and look at the chickadees,
the red belly downies in the bird feeder. To sit back.

To not try so hard. Can someone fail for trying
too hard? To wear my best clothes. To walk tall.

To practice a new song in the garden while weeding
the strawberry patch. To learn an old prayer.

These are the only things we can pack for the journey:
songs, praises, poems, prayers learned by heart.

At Least We Don't Have to Self-Isolate
from Trees

At least we don't have to self-isolate from trees.
In autumn the child loves to stand in the wind

and run to catch leaves. She scans
the backyard for deer and charges at them

to see who backs down first. At least we don't have to
self-isolate from trees. I live by the window

where the maple tree exudes optimism.
It's raining. I brewed a fresh cup of tea

with basil leaves from the garden.
I bite into my own fear like into an apple.

I still crave my mother's approval.
At least we don't have to self-isolate from trees.

A friend of mine is planning to cut down
her apple tree because bears come to steal the apples,

destroy the fence. Meanwhile, I pray for my fruit trees
to bear fruit. We buy apples transported

from thousands of miles away instead of growing them
in the garden. I miss the fences from home.

Controlled by squirrels, woodchucks, and deer.
At least we don't have to self-isolate from trees.

Social-Distancing Fear

Which do you like better? Apples or donuts?
Pears or jelly beans? Badgering or pestering?

My daughter follows me around with
questions. Which do you like better? Optimism

or telling the truth, positivity or reality?
On TV, women show off a new plastic surgery

every season. They look like a commercial
for hair dos and tight tops. Who hangs out

around the house dressed like that? The hour spent
on hair tresses, the trace of the curling iron.

Fake nails, fake eyelashes, they lounge
and sip wine, talk with their friends.

We steel ourselves for winter, don't visit anyone,
don't plan playdates. Which do you like better?

Faltering confidence or looming despair?
Olive bread or no carbs? Chocolate-chip cookies

or celery sticks? Enough already with the food porn pictures
of medium-rare steak and caramel cake on social media.

My sister writes to me on WhatsApp to ask if it's true
that people are waiting in line for free food

around Thanksgiving somewhere in Texas.
It was always true. Which do you like better?

Ordering stuff you don't need online or donating
some canned goods? The wounded silence

of those who linger in the window, alone.

How to Grow a Peach Tree Out of a Pit

Peaches and apricots are the only trees you can grow
from the pit and expect them to stay true.

Saving the pits from our favorite peaches,
I keep them in the fridge for a month

so they think it's winter and then I plant them in pots
and in the yard, carefully marking the spot.

Before you know it, the whole garden will become
a peach orchard, enough fruit for deer, squirrels,

birds, and slugs. Wry comments will fall to the wayside,
and so will the unrelenting grief of avoidance.

Before you know it, neighbors will find peach trees
in their own yards. Squirrels and birds who dig up

the pits will carry them to the meadows. The whole
town will relish the view of the small trees,

delicate tendrils. The narrower the streets in the city,
the more likely the peach trees will survive

because deer won't venture. Before you know it,
fears will dissipate and people will learn to love

fruit trees in their yards again. So ferocious is my devotion
to fruit trees, that I could carry tiny trees on my back

on Main Street and plant them by the front windows.
Winter will tighten down on its resolve.

During lean years, children will peer outside with woeful eyes
only to discover a blossoming tree blossoming.

Momentum

When we moved, only a couple of streets down,
I wanted to bring the compost. Not the plastic bin

but the good stuff that looked like ricotta cheese.
Then I thought of my new-to-me car with tan,

silky fabric seats. So I left the compost behind,
missed it when I planted the new garden: currants

and gooseberries would have loved it. At the new house
we started a new compost: coffee grounds,

tea bags, apple cores. It never seemed like a chore, but like
a ceremony: broccoli and brightness, leaves and regrets,

celery and celebration. At night, my dreams reconfigured
peels of sweet potatoes and butter squash, joy and abandon.

Peach pits and optimism. Grace and gratitude
keep a dream from curdling into a nightmare.

Detritus, debris, flotsam. The threshold between
nourishment and obesity. What does the inside

of the abdomen look like? Yellow omentum.
The moment when, beaming with pride

about our organic garden, I discovered
the pesticide flags on the lawn of our next-door neighbor.

What Is Your Favorite Kind of Apple?

I buy seven kinds of apples at the local store: Honey Crisp,
Ever Crisp, Rome, Empire, Cortland, Tango, Ginger Gold.

My favorite is Jonagold, but they're out. All local apples.
We play a game, line them on the counter for a taste test,

an apple fest. What is your favorite apple?
What does it remind you of? My grandfather grafted

apple trees. One tree had three kinds of apples.
I call my mother to ask if she remembers their names.

All the apple trees he has grafted remain. My father
planted summer apple trees, *mere văratice,*

that ripen first. Having enough apples
for the neighborhood kids. The bruised apples

on the ground go into apple cider. We close our eyes
and try an apple slice, guess which one of the seven.

Would I know? If somebody brought me an apple
from home, like the yellow ones my grandfather planted,

would I recognize it? This Christmas, instead of a sweater,
I should give away an apple tree from a local nursery.

I should give a bushel of apples to a college kid
for her week of final exams. Planting an apple tree

reminds me of where I have traveled,
tethers me to this fruitful, faithful home.

Haircuts in the Backyard

My husband combs our daughter's hair in our garden
then trims it. He is precise and gentle.

When my turn comes, he measures to check if even.
Though fading off, the red dye's still strong. The gray

comes through. I color it myself, refuse to pay
the thousand dollars it would cost a year

to get it done at the salon. Coloring it at home
makes the house stink with toxic chemicals,

makes me nauseated. I've frittered away my youth.
How much time did I spend fiddling with my hair?

When I catch a glimpse of myself in the mirror
I see my mother. I worry she will say I look old.

My husband combs my hair in our garden.
Besides our daughter, in Adirondack chairs,

my grandmothers and great-grandmothers have joined us,
their long, gray hair shining, rinsed with walnut leaves.

They look fierce and vulnerable. Unrelenting,
never unmoored during famine, wars, poverty—or Covid.

Should I Learn How to Knit Socks?

Should I learn how to knit socks? Unspool unbidden
memories. Maybe I don't remember some of my dreams

but knitting socks will summon back my grandmother
lying down on my lap for me to scratch her head.

Should I learn how to knit socks? It will probably take me
at least forty hours. Who has forty hours? As if someone

tied my hands so I can't do anything else. At least
I wouldn't buy anything online. You can't

knit socks and click "Place order now" at the same time.
At least I wouldn't be snacking. You can't knit socks

and eat pumpkin pie at the same time. At least I wouldn't
be scrolling down on my phone. You can't knit socks

and tweet at the same time. All the bad habits I cannot
succumb to while knitting socks. For thousands of years,

women knitted socks by the fire. Both of my grandmothers,
with all the women who came before me, would tell me

to go outside and play with my daughter, run a kite.
When we tire, we can sit together and learn

how to knit socks, find some old pictures stashed away
in a dusty box, disentangle the threads of old stories.

My Mother Says I Would Have Found a Job in Romania

To tell you the truth I always feel guilty for leaving home.
I'm sure I would have found a job in Romania.

I measure the distance from New York to Bucharest
in miles, hours from door to door: the luxury of leisure

on the plane, the layovers. The expense. But also—my daughter
doesn't want to go to Romania anymore. To tell you the truth,

ninety percent of my dreams at night are set in Romania,
so maybe that means that although I have lived in the States

for twenty-seven years, at night my subconscious lavishes
in the farmer's market in Focşani and buys freesias

and tuberoses. To tell you the truth, the hardest
is imagining my mother sequestered in her apartment

on the fifth floor. We see each other on WhatsApp.
She shows me new jars of pickled bell peppers,

pickled mushrooms, eggplant chutneys and tapenade.
The longer we stay on the phone, the more we set the threads

for a tapestry for me to weave all night long.
We listen and linger. The deepening labor of loneliness

notwithstanding, my mother demurs and dallies.
She tells me about a fire in Piatra Neamţ

at a Covid intensive-therapy unit:
many dead, some patients saved by their doctor.

How Many Trees Have You Planted?

When you buy a new house, do you
dig out the cherry tree and the red pear trees

you have just planted last August? How much
would you pay for a sour-cherry tree?

Some say sour-cherry juice is good for sleeping.
If you can't sleep you shouldn't dig out fruit trees.

How many trees have you grafted?
Did you give away cuttings from your plants?

Did you become a library of seeds?
Did you dig out the lawn to sow

wildflowers and seduce the bees?
What did you spray on your lawn?

Some of us plan to leave gold to our children.
Some of us leave debt to our children.

Some of us plant trees for our children,
invest in pear trees, fall in love with apricot trees.

A student in my class says he has never
eaten a plum. Tomorrow, we should take to school

some organic fruit. We should leave fruit trees
for our children. Forget about diamonds.

Teach them how to treat a fruit tree
before it catches some disease. Our garden,

suffused by the buzz of drunk bees. Our spring,
a dance of dandelions, a reckoning of trees.

What I Lost

Unwieldy, the night laughs at me, sends me notice
from those who loved me, but I misread the signs.

When I was a child, my mother used to leave me
for the whole summer with my grandparents.

As she walked away, I followed her on the inside
of the garden, she on the outside, and I cried.

So did I learn to let go by not letting go. So did I learn
to win by not winning. When I left the country

at twenty-two for graduate school, she didn't want me to go.
She knew I wasn't coming back, the way mothers

know the story before it begins. Twenty-seven years later,
I haven't learned anything my mother hasn't already

told me. I waded through worry, begrudged the cost.

The Enchantment of Houses

I wanted to paint all the rooms white, to remind me
of the houses in our mountains, the houses I left behind

with their quince trees and lilies-of-the-valley.
My mother usually whitewashed the whole house.

Sometimes in spring she got into a cleaning frenzy
and scrubbed the house from corner to corner,

one room at a time. These days I don't want to move.
All I want is to sit by the window, drink a cup of tea,

and dream of all the places I shouldn't have left.
Instead of replaying the movie of old houses,

I should acknowledge that all houses look the same
as long as I settle down and dissolve the fear.

All I need is to bring along a small icon, learn
a new prayer by heart and write my own prayer.

Rain in the Garden

I have placed enough chairs in the love garden
so welcome spirits can linger and lounge,
relax and listen, maybe try the sweet peas.
Think of someone you should have slept with

when you were young. But you didn't.
Rain is like that. Keep the phone away
in another room. Sadness seeps in
through the charger: if you tiptoe around the house

and unplug every device, rain will wash away
the malaise. Rain is like eating eclairs
without the eclairs. Like news without the farce.
Rain is like having enough food in the house

on a Saturday afternoon, socially distanced
from the rest of the world, none of us
zonked out in front of Netflix. Tablets
abandoned. Yesterday, instead of mulch,

I laid down newspapers around the tomatoes.
As I covered the front page with old maple leaves,
I spotted another story about a sixteen-year old
murdered downtown, body cameras off.

Prayer for an Apricot Tree

In Romanian, apricots are feminine, grapes masculine,
and apples neuter. Gender is a matter of language.

The apricot tree deliberates whether to come back to life,
a dormant tree shipped across the country in June.

Every morning when I water it, I check to see if a green leaf
has broken. Abiding respect for trees that return.

Even the roots were trimmed down, bare. The chance journey
of trees that travel from a nursery across the country.

Does the tree learn my name, recognize my voice?
The warning of things that burn. The floorboards

in the living room. My chair, the windowsill.
Are they still alive? Do they still remember?

The triumph of an apricot tree that takes. I ordered it online,
a one-year warranty, but I would have to ship it back

if it dies and I don't see myself going to the post office
with a packed dead stick. Shipping back a dead tree.

I remember all the trees my father planted.
He picked apricots, laid them out in the good room

and saved them for us. The longest it's been
since I didn't go home is four years.

In two months, since we moved to this new house,
we have planted eleven fruit trees, including two figs.

Slowly, our garden is coming alive. Slowly, I learn to open
the gifts passed down to me. Slowly, I learn to share the fruit.

November after Elections

Nights, longer. Light, dimmer. Tea, weak.
Go for long walks despite the frost.

Friends, stunned. Countenance, desolate.
Knit a sweater out of hair and feathers like a nest

for the one person who is the loneliest
this late November. Clouds, low.

The best haven't turned on the furnace yet.
Scarred with mold, the unseen side of the wall.

Will, receding. Plans, derelict. Lists, abandoned.
Left the stems of the flowers up

and all the brush, so bees and bugs can winter,
and deer can scavenge for shoots and sap.

Loners sludge through Mondays,
eat their way through endless afternoons

at the office, chewing on some desiccated
unrecognizable bar. So far, nobody

notices who is lost, who is absent,
who is locked in, who is locked out.

Rituals

I want to call my friend and tell her
to place an open bottle of red wine
and a large pretzel, *colac,* above the door,

to leave them there for forty days
so the spirit can come home
and feast.

I want to tell her to carry a bucket
of water to the grave of her husband
every day for forty days.

I want to tell her to leave one light on
in the house
for forty nights.

I want to tell her to give away
one sweater, one shirt, one hat
to all of his friends

until all his clothes are gone,
to start with their sons,
keeping a blue flannel shirt for herself.

I want to tell her to ask all their friends
to give away food, books, plates,
and to say "In this world, may it be

for your soul;
in the other world,
may it be for Murray's soul."

But, instead, I translate a prayer
from Romanian, and repeat it
till I fall asleep.

White Porch

The snow has veered off to elsewhere,
careened to another space. Despite the cold,

my father is offering Murray
mulled wine (red wine, three pepper corns

and a teaspoon of sugar brought to a boil
until it foams and the aroma fills the house).

They are sitting outside on the porch
and tell each other stories. My father

is wearing his *șubă,* an overcoat
made out of lamb's wool, with a wide collar

and his sheepskin hat. He died
when he was 64, twelve years ago,

Murray at 74, less than a month ago,
so they are only two years apart,

but my father has been in the other world
longer, so he welcomes him

like a host. They sit on my porch
and sip their hot wine out of large mugs

my mother gave away for my father's soul.
They eat *covrigi* and *colaci,* woven

bread and pretzels. My father
has apples and smoked veal

on a Romanian plate.
All these years, my mother

has been sending him food
by giving it away to someone poor.

They laugh. Murray has large eyes,
not believing what the other world is like.

He wants to tell me, so I don't fear.
They are talking, but I can't hear

their words. I can see the steam
from their hot wine that doesn't get cold

the way my mother gave it away for his soul.
My father knows that I'm fine.

Every time I miss him I send something
to my mother or I give her a call

especially when snow divulges
winter's secrets of trust,

a storm swirls in the neighborhood,
and friends huddle around the table.

Scarce Temptations

During communism we were not allowed to try clothes on
before buying them. We went to a store

and the assistant looked with disdain, almost refused
to give us the dress, barely let us touch the silk.

If we bought it, we could never return it—
buying something was as final as an arranged marriage:

we took the dress home and prayed for the best.
We only bought one outfit per year, and when we got home

we learned to take it in or let the seams out. My mother
would fret till she found new shoes and then wouldn't step

close to a shop. Even when we wanted to buy,
there wasn't much—halls echoed. Mirrors turned green.

Today, shelves are stacked, but my mother has given up,
says we'd have to chase her to go to a store.

The Garden after Elections

Putting the garden to sleep, I pulled out the tomato plants,
took away the trellises for cucumbers and green beans.

Three days after the election, people were learning Math
and gawked to realize 46% of those eligible to vote

didn't. The kale was surviving vigorously, but some
green bugs had invaded it and laid eggs,

so we couldn't eat it, although the shoots were young
and strong, and would have made some perfect

chips in just five minutes in the oven. I struggled
to stay away from the computer, tried to avoid

turning on the TV. The people I overheard
were on the other side, though some denied.

The freesias I planted the first of May finally emerged,
already too late. Soon it would snow and the flowers

would not resist, so I transplanted them in pots,
attending to each plant till dusk, so I could stay outside.

They Knit the Truth

They got their walking sticks,
their head scarves, their hand-knit

cardigans in brown or black,
aprons over their skirts, as they sit

outside their gates. They don't wonder
whose turn it is. Anyone is fair game

at this point. One hundred, ninety,
even sixty-four. They walk,

make their own meals, sleep
with their doors open.

They laugh and exchange recipes
about tea. Bouquets of John's Wort,

chamomile, and sage are drying
by the eaves. As for thieves,

they find nothing to steal.
Finally, old women

can say what they want,
do as they please, watch

from the porch as younger
women fret, worry, appease

those who have power.
Meanwhile, the old women

knit, spin, and weave
because now they know.

Everyday Rituals

My mother walks to one store
to buy a dark, whole-wheat loaf of bread
baked in a brick oven,

to another store the other direction
to buy a small packet of butter
so it stays fresh,

to the farmers market
for cherries, and checks all the aisles first
before buying from an old woman from the mountains.

She hurries to a place
in another part of town
to buy a bottle of milk

the kind that only lasts one day
and she has to test it at home in a spoon on the open flame
to see if it turned.

Everything is fresh and organic,
as if it were for a child's first food
or for an ailing aunt in the hospital.

This takes her hours in the morning,
before climbing to her apartment on the fifth floor
and resting her tired feet

as if all of it were some kind of gym
and therapy, a dance she has mastered—
no tickets, no audience, no special lights.

III

Prostrations

After Pierre Auguste Renoir "Study, Torso, Sunlight Effect"

We should all have an artist paint our portrait
before we get to the point of refusing to wear

sleeveless shirts. We should all have a gifted
photographer take pictures of us that make us look

like a Renoir model. When we turn eighty-seven—
should we all be so lucky to turn eighty-seven,

we will look back on the way we looked today
and wish we understood we were all right.

Painters teach us it's all about the light:
if only we could capture the light. Blue

diffused through blue. Hospitality of trust,
of loving eyes. Mutual adoration of colors.

Recognizing someone: an icon of luminescence.
Every morning realizing sanctity:

the beauty of the beloved. Resisting
gerontophobia: the older you are today

the more I remember in you the summer
of ripeness, the tall, proud posture

of feeling at home in your confidence.
Eternally grateful for your steps.

The round gestures of your kindness.
The wisdom of your calm. Content.

The Things We Cannot Keep

After Matisse, "Annelisse with White Tulips and Anemones"

What we collect, what we accumulate.
And yet the things we cannot keep—

flowers, seasons, beloved who go away.
The acerbic gaze that struggles to save

from the deceit of time. The grace we choose
to sustain: in the painting, flowers don't wither.

In my eyes, you will always stay young,
you never get sarcastic, brittle, wry.

The courage to let go of things, the strength
not to buy things, not to trade your time

for clutter that fills the space, multiplies
on shelves, makes the air hard to breathe

with debris and dust. The secret is always
not who pays the bill for all the detritus,

but who cleans, who keeps the look sparse.
Records of resilience, the triumph of resisting

the assailing pressure of want. The strength
of walking in the narrow aisles of a store

and holding back: I have already fallen in love
so I don't need to buy things anymore.

We Live in Paradise

After Thomas Cole, "Catskill Mountain House: The Four Elements"

Painters decide the landscape of a culture.
Their images, icons of a generation—

what painters see we see. Furious as fire,
riveting as the river, the view of the valley. We need

to see the collections of paintings to realize
the beauty of this place. To taste the wisdom

of looking, the song of landscape, the whispers
of the water. Every house hides its own demise,

every friend arrives with a promise. We love
so deeply because we understand the incidence

of elements: what miracle that in this lifetime
I see you! What ecstasy to hide the depth

of my devotion! To worship trees, to speak
the language of romance, to grapple

with the gravity of grammar. In our house,
we will always listen, learn instruments,

embrace the mathematics of prayer,
the symmetry of song, the forbidden taste

of summer. Dance of delight, music of murmurs—
what escapes, what triumphs, what remains.

Your portrait, an aura of kindness. The view,
the adoring gaze, synchronized steps, your halo.

Portraits

After Robert Henry, "Luxembourg Gardens, Stormy Sky"

Sometimes, we forget what mattered. How beautiful
you looked, till we see an old picture that reminds us

that we should have believed in the balance. Indelible,
the steps. The responsibility of memory. My job

is to tell the story, to help others remember the struggle.
To bear witness, to recreate the likeness of that day.

To make lists. What have we omitted, neglected?
Clouds brought out one's truth. Did we recognize

those who stayed? The subtle peace of pacing,
the path to tenderness. Discerning who brings the clouds.

Embracing lean months. Avoiding the deceptive words
of chronic puppeteers. Setbacks tighten the resolve.

The hours of sitting by the water are short, the echoes
everlasting, should we only grapple with the sloping

summers of what we left behind. The liability
of lingering. Perceiving the limp pretexts of liars.

Golden Geometry of Light

After Wolf Kahn, "Saltbox Barn in an Open Field" (2003)

The calm and peace of proportion
before the world spirals: accepting

the gifts of the eye. Evading marathons.
Glimpses of glow. Not to want, not to wish,

not to regret. Without anyone seeing, the world
imparts the secret of symmetry. Every house

is a temple, a church, an altar. With every sign,
to discern or to miss. A revelation snaps into place

only to disappear again, forgotten,
with the persistent creed of trees.

The equilibrium of light conceals
as it discloses. Home means understanding

a lesson, taking a piece of advice.
Arresting intuition. Comforting care.

Resisting the cadging temptations
of idleness. Strength is made of hope,

the way composure is made of summer,
illuminations of yellow and green.

The Return of Sauntering

After Claude Monet, "Boulevard de Capucines"

From the window, the world is always more incisive,
sagacious. To fall in love with strangers in a painting.

The pure art of people watching. After social distancing,
to board an airplane again, to go to the theater, to step

into a classroom again. Music of blue colors,
elegance of silhouettes, superior pleasure

of knowing how to wear a hat. Every day
to fall in love with generosity. Even winter

boasts its fruits: all the waiting has paid off
and nobody can foil the futility of resistance. The joy

of embracing old friends, even only in thought.
Quick steps on a crisp morning: how to adore

even your lassitude, even your lethargy, even
your lollygagging. Or your brisk balance,

your courageous retina. To comprehend
the contours of your perfection. Wise as to see.

Notwithstanding

After Frederic Edwin Church, "Above the Clouds at Sunrise"

Easy to adore, like the mathematics of framing a painting,
where everything falls into place. The countenance

of contentment. A master has planned every detail:
symmetry of summer. In good time, learn to decipher

the perfection of the present that surpasses the plan.
In good time, learn to effect systemic change. Today,

we hold out hope that grammar will offer respite. Today,
we hold out hope that the clouds will rise. Respect

the guest who lingers, who sits on the steps. Respect
the inscrutable signs of peace. Recognize the neighbor's

pain, the quiet wisdom, what is left unsaid. The silence
of sorrow. What if suspicions are wrong?

Goldfinches are here; hummingbirds are here—
kindness nowhere to be found? Send to your great-

grandchildren a healthy orchard. Keep bees
for your beloved, carry baskets of cherries

as gifts to the ailing. Give away the first apricots
and the last. The more persecuted you are,

the more beloved. The more mistreated,
the more understood. Don't dash the dreams,

don't disturb the dawn: devotion, offering,
sacrifice. Respect the revered strength of friends,

who persevere, staunch in their beliefs,
who remain standing notwithstanding deceit.

I Have Already Read the Book

After Helen Greene Blumenschein, "Summer"

The illumination of days. The revelation. How does one
waste the light? Sleep is a song in which rhyme

brings together my father, who plays chess with my uncle
and their uncles in the other world. Dream is a melody

in which my great-grandchildren are waiting, nourished
by the organic amaranth of my faith. The harvest

of my hurry. Precipitous like rain. Stay with me tonight,
and be my guest. I will make for you a lavish meal

of quinoa and quest. I will bathe your feet. I will
welcome you with mangoes and raspberries,

apricots and figs. I will always remember
your kindness, your generosity, your loyalty.

The night is the treasure of memory: the paths
on your palms. The smile alone, years afterwards.

Hidden, what I was too busy to see,
too harried to go along for a lark. The spark

in your eye, the wicked confidence of your swagger:
what you know, you already know.

Why do I worry when I have already read the book—
I still haven't read the book.

Can We Always Honor a Promise?

After Albert Bierstadt, "Mount Washington with Huntington's Ravine"

I was there. As if I was never there. The mountain
of discontent. I breathed in and I listened, inspired

by the air in my lungs. I fell in love with your lungs.
I fell in love with the river of your riveting innuendoes.

I fell in love with the arch of your feet, with your toes
and your torso. I fell in love with your halo,

the echo of your words, your laughter, your laughter,
your laughter. I heard you cry and I listened.

I heard you cry and I didn't decipher what you asked me.
The answer was already there but I didn't know

the question. I was there. As if I was never there.
I saw and I felt with my fingers. The valley

smelled of incense and lemon verbena. It smelled
of green pines. It smelled of the most secret

memory. An intimation of immortality. A sign.
Will you promise me to remember? Write it down.

The Fish Will Always Tell the Truth

After Jonas Lie, "On the Wings of the Morning"

Paradise reveals itself in the morning when I wake up
to listen to the birds. Cold water, blue of green.

Every time I wash my face, I remember your smile,
the sparkle of your light. The quiet stir of dawn.

How I welcome your story. How I listen to the lull
in the litany. The grace of guidance. Give me

the superb wisdom to understand the miracle
of your presence. Give me gratitude to see

the divine sign of the burden you shoulder,
the oppression you dispel. If I could stand tall.

If I could honor your generosity. If I could keep
the water clean. If I could honor the water.

If I could learn to listen to the water. You are more
handsome than honeycombs, more honorable

than beekeepers, more hardworking than farmers,
more hopeful than teachers, more truthful than fish.

You Knew All Along

After Lucius Richard O'Brian, "Sunrise on the Saguenay"

Chasing the light despite the asymmetry
of blessings: when you do a good deed, someone

will pray for you when you sleep. Effective
therapy: sending money to those in need

when they don't expect it. Waking up at five AM
to water the fruit trees in scorching July.

Taking pictures of dresses for your sister
till she chooses one. How much time

have you wasted in fear rather than giving
what someone asks for, not what you want?

Always longing for the horizon rather than
listening to the litany of bird song.

Always dreaming of traveling elsewhere.
Gestures that anchor. Gifts that express

recognition, gratitude, glee—
seeing, knowing all along. Mirroring.

Orchards and Wilderness

If my great-grandmothers could see us, what would
they tell me to do with my days? Would they approve

of the debt unpaid? What deeds would they want me to do?
What words to withhold? How did they spend their days?

How did they resist? How did they speak up? How
did they help others? How did they welcome strangers,

show hospitality? Elsewhere, there were castles,
but my grandmothers toiled, struggled, survived.

I wish they had written down what they learned.
I wish they had written down what I should do.

Maybe they tell me and I don't know how to read
the signs. The days lag. The loss laments.

Tell me what I should give you. I will lavish you
with my time. I will listen, lean in, and lend

to you what I needed when I was young.
I will save the bees for you. I will mail to you

orchards and wilderness. I will lease
a piece of land and plant pollinators,

bring birds and butterflies. I will send to you in time
how much I loved you, how much I prayed.

The Romanian Blouse

After all these years, I still don't own an embroidered
Romanian blouse. I have some ancient ones woven

and sewn by my grandmothers or my mother,
but I don't wear any of the new ones, copies

designed to look like the authentic ones.
I guess I cannot walk around with a museum piece.

When one of my friends traveled through Romania,
he bought woven carpets, embroidered scarves.

At the end of the trip, on his way out, the hosts
threw in "this tattered rug." Their treasure—

they didn't know. Sometimes we give away
what we love most, not what others want. Over the years

I gave away old pieces of embroidery or glazed
ceramic plates. Every embroidered Romanian blouse,

every plate I have carried back across the ocean. Every *ie*
will clothe my soul in the other world. Here,

the *ie* yellows in boxes downstairs. Chronic
allergies to dust. Stuffed closets. Count

how many tops you own. Why? What desire
pushes you to keep searching? Is all you want

always elsewhere? Already here? Cheap
imitations. Ambiguity. Elusive blue of chicory.

Ștefan Luchian's Flowers

My pet peeve is a vase that does not hold water.
An impractical vase that does not hold flowers.

A vase not designed to hold the weight of flowers.
A poem that does not rhyme. When we moved, I found

twenty vases in the house. When I look at Ștefan Luchian's
paintings, I want the flowers, I want the vase.

I want to plant Ștefan Luchian's flowers. I want to learn
how to paint watercolors to paint his flowers.

I want to take pictures of vases of flowers. I want to ask
my sister to buy for me a vase and even imagine

sending her a picture of the vase I want. I want
an album of Luchian's paintings of flowers.

I want to go home to buy a vase,
go to the *Muzeul Național de Artă al României*

from Calea Victoriei in Bucharest. I want to go home
this summer. I want to go home every summer.

Don't send me flowers. I only adore the flowers
I grow in my garden, possibly from seed. Flowers

I waited and prayed for. Don't send me stuff
I don't want. He painted flowers, house bound.

Patterns

My grandmother took the cows to the pasture
and carried on her back freshly-cut hay.

Not once did she sleep in, always up to feed them
at dawn. She carried water in buckets on a *cobiliță,*

a wood pole that cut through her shoulder bone.
She set cheese in ancient patterns

carved out of wood shaped like a star
inside a circle. Chicory, the sun, or the eye.

The wood patterns left their imprint on both sides
of the wheel. She never took a break.

Nobody gave her any accolades. Her phrases
she left with me are pure poetry: "When I die,

you'll find this garden deserted," or "Men are only
good to stick their balls between two stones

and crush them." She wove, stitched sequins on shirts
and scarves for her son's wedding, who never

got married. Nobody is wearing them now. Nobody
praises them. Today, I want to go back and find

the wood patterns before the old house
collapses, before mold and rain lay claim.

Ghazal for the Path Home

By leaving home, I learned not to look in the mirror
because the lake hides the truth in its mirror.

My mother said a horse came in the garden. I told her
not to fix the fence. To bring more horses like a mirror.

Last evening, a deer gave birth to a fawn in the thicket
we let grow in the back of our garden to mirror

the lack of wilderness in our neighborhood. Since then
we saw rabbits and foxes. A bear—a mirror

for the magnificence of the night. Summer plays the violin.
The garden brings all the birds who look at us like a mirror.

My daughter cries that we refuse to get her a dog,
and so every day I fail to fulfil a promise, mirror.

I remember when I was a child my mother protected me
against a vicious dog. My mother's face is my mirror.

Many journeys have I taken. The path home
has remained the only way to look in the mirror.

Rosa Damascena

I watch a short film about the Bulgarian rose.
I don't speak Bulgarian and I have never traveled there

although it would have been so close. Why have I not asked
the right questions? Why did I not listen more?

Now I want to travel. The trucks heaving down the street
bring packages and people fill their basements.

I want a *Rosa Damascena* with edible roses.
I want to make *Rosa Damascena* syrup,

Rosa Damascena ice pops, *Rosa Damascena*
Romanian preserves the way I tried them at home.

Travel with me home this summer. Take a teaspoon
of *Rosa Damascena* preserves with a glass of cold

water freshly brought from the well, the way
my grandmother served them to me when I was a child.

Language and Maps

Of all the places on this earth, how many have I seen?
We travel in summer and face the questions

and promises of thresholds. Every day
I learn to forgive. Every day I beg to be forgiven

for trying too hard, for not trying enough.
Of all the languages I tried to learn, how many words

do I remember? Mysteries of dusk, revelations
of conjunctions, which hold grammar and fish together

suspended in the molasses of postponing. Tomorrow
I will buy tickets for another country. Tomorrow

I will brush on a language I won't use. Have you noticed
how in your dreams you're always fluent and confident—

or terrified? Purified? I wish I had traveled more,
seen my friends more. My friend, invite me over

to see your country. Wait for me at the airport,
make for me a simple meal of hardy bread,

a cup of soup. My friend, I will do the same for you.
I will always wait for you. I will always honor you.

I will listen to your stories, bring toys for your children,
cardigans for your mother. I will always remember

what you looked like when you were young,
I will always laugh with you—and I will wash your feet.

The Chronic Confidence of Want

Around that house, I am more me. Quickened language
of palimpsests. Lace curtains, broken windows.

My family is deciding whether to sell my grandparents'
crumbling house. Maybe two rooms could be saved.

More expensive to demolish than to buy new.
Someone found a horse roaming in the garden.

We should fix the fence to keep out the horse—
or bring more horses so no one has to mow.

The weeds grow trunks like trees. One day
we cry about selling the house. No buyers.

Why would I want a house in another country—
I haven't been to Romania in three years. The other

grandchildren don't claim it. My uncle planted
apple trees. At night, the rain pelts

through the broken roof. I frittered away my days.
Half of my dreamwork happens in that house. Why

have I left? The graininess of the painting. Mold,
dust, mice. They gave away the two dogs he got

only six months before. His cats now feral, famished.
We lock the door to a collapsing house—

so it doesn't fall on anyone. Chronic confidence
of want. Across the ocean, my apple tree.

Fighting the Urge to Clean

Scrub the floor, walls, bathroom tiles.
Clean the windows with rumpled newspapers
the way my mother did,
she on the inside and I on the balcony outside—
we scrubbed the windows with vinegar
and the glass squeaked. We saw our faces,
my mom driving the house by sheer will.
I would have sat down with a book but her whirlpool
seized the house, a torrent of will sharp like steel.

Bleach the grout, wipe the backsplash.
Soap the fruit tray and the vegetable tray
in the fridge and the dirt syrup trapped on the shelves.
Throw out every useless gadget,
every antiquated cord from some electronics
we discarded a long while ago.

Scour until my fingers prune inside the gloves
and the smell of peroxide sinks in, too much
for pores, too much for breathing.
Launder and fold until the house is spinning,
the closet filled with neat piles of color-coordinated
tops and cardigans, reds and whites and purples.

Clean till my fingers bleed, cuticles
shredded, curled back the way my mother
washed the clothes by hand, rough sheets
she rubbed with home-made soap
she had boiled in a cauldron in summer.
And then she put all the clothes on the line
outside. The skin on her hands swollen
and thinned at the same time.

Or I could fight the urge to clean,
make a fresh cup of tea—and burn that draft.

"He Wore the Shirt You Sent Him"

Sometimes I buy shirts in my father's size,
so when I give them away, I am sending them

to him. When I was a child, the women in the mountains
used to say, "don't accept food from a stranger,

or from an envious woman—don't accept anything
from them." But the gifts you receive from someone

who loves you back will protect you like in that fairy tale,
"The Six Swans," where a sister knits shirts

for her brothers. I have woven my love into this shirt
I am sending to you with hope and faith,

so it will serve as your shield to protect you
of fear and loneliness, of hunger and despair,

of cold and doubt, of poverty and drought.

Return

I dredged the river of my childhood,
cajoled every voice, pressed every drop

of juice out of silence. Confidence
was an orchard in the sun, rays

revealing the shiny plumpness of apples.
Ripe. Ready. Like a ritual, every gesture

was its own reward, like the return
of the father in the sunset,

who was walking home
bringing a round loaf of bread

and a bottle of red wine as if nothing
had happened. As if he didn't know

how long he'd been gone, his eyes
lit up: he liked what he saw.

Organic Flowers from My Garden

Like having a vase of flowers on the table,
the day is all yours, to read the book.

What have you given away today? How many
books have you read? Break a mirror. I take that back.

Dust a mirror. Dusting is worse than laundry:
I take that back: dusting and laundry

are a form of love when your child is allergic
to dust. Forgive me for not doing enough.

Forgive me for not dusting enough.
Forgive me for breathing. Forgive me for not being

younger. Forgive me for not being older. Kindness
is a form of sanctity. Music

is a form of blossoming apple trees. Apricots
are a form of compassion. Lollygagging

is a form of wisdom. Your handwriting
is a form of faith. I balk at lethargy

and languor. When you buy flowers from the store,
where do they come from? What plump

poison has been pumped into them
to bring them? From what country? How many miles

have they traveled around the world?
Who planted and picked them?

What were they paid? What did they put
in the ground? What did they put in the water?

What did they spray on them to keep the bugs
away? What did they do to the bees?

Tell me when you want me to bring to you
a bouquet of purple gladiolas, delphinium, and blue bells

from my organic garden. (Forgive me that my neighbors
spray heavy pesticides, their lawn lush, putrid.)

Your Friends from Around the World

Invite your friends to your hometown, explain the real
story, the truth behind every statue, the local theater.

Become a history guide. Recite poems you learned by heart
in your native language when you were a kid.

Stroll in front of every water fountain. Share
old pictures of your favorite shirt from high school,

introduce them to your retired teachers
who play chess on a bench in the park,

grandmas wearing black dresses
mourning the passing of their youth.

Give your guests candles to light in the cathedral,
show them the temple, the mosque.

More inspiring and less afraid, more generous
and less anxious. Step into a used bookstore,

mail a dozen postcards, buy a coffee-table album
of the most beloved painter of your county,

play a rhapsody on the old violin.
Hosting guests from around the world:

proof that God exists. Your friends' feet
in dusty sandals hold up the sky.

The Table of Your Generosity

What is ignored, what I didn't see: you were always there,
smiling, listening, welcoming, with your arms open.

You believed in sunshine, in the color blue.
You believed in kindness. You remembered old stories

and knew how to retell them so even the stones listened.
You saw people, loved them, asked questions that made

them remember who they were, who you were. A mirror,
you gave back the silhouette, the liking, the profile.

You accepted every prodigal soul. Made glory out of sky.
Made summer out of a glass of water. Generous,

like the light in the morning, you brought back hope,
relief, optimism. You reminded us about the eternal

youth of dance and welcomed every stranger.
Your table, a sculpture of giving and grace.

In Confidence

After Asher B. Durand, "Woodland Interior" (1850)

Who can afford to walk alone
in the woods?

Cradle of green and patience:
summer muddles through heat,

slopes through comfort,
spins a cocoon of intimacy.

August clings to the skin,
closeup of trust and peace.

Dismisses the demands of the day.
Wistful like the attraction

of a new season streaming.
Forest bathing. Planting trees.

Celestial long walks:
do trees hold hands?

Oversized armchairs of moss,
pillows, blankets, nests of softness.

Do trees fall in love?
Initiation into the name of trees.

Restlessness and its cure.
Confidence of not knowing.

Finding out the truth
and not being allowed to tell.

Reading the signs. Longing
for home and escaping home.

Father, Don't Call Me Home

After Childe Hassam, "Celia Thaxter's Garden" (Isle des Shoals, Maine 1890)

When the world is tranquil
you don't even know—smooth

and giddy like gladioli.
Through the intercession of flowers,

the revelation of peace.
Contentment. Calm.

Plant zinnias by the road,
so the passersby can see them.

Plant mock orange by the water—
imagine the symmetry,

the equilibrium of summer.
Father, don't call me home.

I want to walk by the river,
incite my grandchildren to tell stories,

spoil them with apricots,
let them loose in the strawberry patch.

I only have what I give to you.
Letters from home welcome.

Goldfinch pirouettes welcome.
Chamomile and rosemary welcome.

Neighbors linger by an invisible fence.
Plant tuberoses as a pretext

to kneel in the garden.
Learn by heart the rhythm of faith.

Learn how to heal fruit trees.
Learn how to heal bees.

Ode to Romanian Old Women

Romanian old women wear *capoate,* black housedresses,
because they're always mourning: another train arrives,

another horse-drawn cart procession, church bells ringing.
Romanian old women wear *capoate* with small chicory,

so cooking stains don't show—from stuffed grape leaves,
wedding soups, roasted roosters, cherry preserves,

juices and sauces that splatter an arduous cook's kitchen.
Romanian old women wear *capoate* with front buttons

all the way down so they can undo them at the knee
when they jump over a fence to grab a stray sheep,

when they skip over a ditch to chase drunk husbands
out of the pub, or when they charge after their sons

with *făcălețul,* the wooden stick for stirring
mămăligă, after catching them with another woman.

Romanian old women wear *capoate* so they can bring
the shamed sons back to the wife with a gurgling baby.

Romanian old women wear nondescript *capoate*
so from the back they all look the same

when they step into a neighbor's garden
to snip some rosemary. Romanian old women

wear *capoate* with front pockets to sneak zinnia seeds
or hide lavender and basil to smell like a bride at the altar.

The Lake of Met Desire

Watching a couple, how they sip each other with their eyes
in public. Electric, a conduit for paradise,

how they flirt, how they praise each other when the other
steps out of the room, how they follow each other

at parties with their gaze, how they check each other
when they think nobody's watching, how they touch

each other's elbows softly. Quick smile just for them,
anticipation of a gesture, surprise unspoken of,

promise fulfilled. Thirsty, they taste each other's words,
foresee each other's needs, startle each other

with eye gifts—how does one know before the self
knows? Mischievous and raucous, forever the same

as on their third date: tingling, magnetic, attracting
everyone else, enmeshing them in the galvanism

of their current, the way the blossoming catnip plant
in the garden attracts drunk bees and goldfinches. Divine,

the couple madly in love after thirty years: for them,
every breakfast is a date on the deck overlooking

the lake of met desire: mirror of their eyes.

Immigrant Verbs

If your beloved friends from your youth forgot about you,
don't worry. After all, living in another part of the world

steals you from friends, like living with no summer.
Make new friends, like chicory. Obdurate, light-blue,

it grows on the side of the road, meeting the eye
of summer, the gold of secrets, dispelling the fears

of travelers and souls forlorn. If old friends gave you up,
pay the water bill for someone in need. Petitionary prayer,

making a new friend means you dig a well
or pay for someone's heating bill in a long winter.

Do not bemoan the loss of old friends: they held your hand
as a guide. Their time with you, the first flutter

of daffodils. Friends are like summer: sweet or somber.
Brew some rosemary tea to keep alive the memory,

to remember the salt of sauntering through an old town
where you know all the streets, all the benches,

best bakeries. Disgruntled or persnickety,
suave or serene, friends who don't write back

are like an adjective you thought was always married
to a noun only to find out that summer

slips into sleepy shades, teaches the tenderness
of new grammar, sleek syllables, sly maps.

The Privilege of Water

When I water the garden in the morning
I also water all the gardens my father has planted

and then he looked up at the sky for months
searching in vain for a sign of rain.

I also water the fields where my grandmothers toiled
with no profit or recognition all their lives.

Water is sacred. It douses my father's wounds
when a tree fell on him when he worked a forestry job

or, later, when he fell off a ladder fixing the roof
of the house he built in his retirement for us to go home.

We didn't go home. What is it about children who leave
and keep away grandchildren from grandparents?

When I water the garden in the morning
I grow a garden of paradise: tomatoes and fig trees,

seven kinds of berries, dozens of kinds of flowers
that remind me of home. If my grandmothers can see me

they recognize the flowers of their youth. They wear
their traditional *ie,* the Romanian blouse, sit in my garden

spinning wool on an ancient distaff and tell stories.
They have sent to me all these flowers—they gave me

their eyes, their hands, the *catrințe,* the woven,
traditional skirts, and the longing for home, *dorul.*

They show me that my garden is a mirror image
of the garden where they are right now with more flowers

than dreams, enough water for parched lips, enough salt,
enough sweet, enough summer, enough rain.

The Miracle of Dawn

After Maximilien Luce, "Quay at Camaret, Finistere"

Welcome morning promises. Before the rest of the world
wakes up, make a list of the splendors of light: hope

at daybreak is like a boat ready to leave as another one
arrives: gifts of faith and reward. The march of summer.

Who is braver: those who prepare to travel far away
or those who see them off, standing to watch them depart?

The dots of every moment: seconds that make up
a necklace of beads. What we take on the journey

and what remains. A sister who leaves. One who waits.
The one who risks it all and the one who prays every night:

somewhere in the world, already aurora. Someone
washes her face, combs her hair in front of the mirror

and tries to save the icon of the second. Somewhere,
my sister looks out of the window, her heart

quickening. Out of breath, she follows a silhouette
in the distance, only to realize it's only a stranger.

About the Author

Lucia Cherciu writes both in English and in Romanian and is the author of six books of poetry, including *Train Ride to Bucharest* (Sheep Meadow Press, 2017), a winner of the Eugene Paul Nassar Poetry Prize; *Edible Flowers* (Main Street Rag, 2015); *Lalele din Paradis / Tulips in Paradise* (Editura Eikon, 2017); *Altoiul Râsului / Grafted Laughter* (Editura Brumar, 2010); and *Lepădarea de Limbă / The Abandonment of Language* (Editura Vinea, 2009).

She served as the 2021–2022 Dutchess County, NY, poet laureate, and her work was nominated multiple times for a Pushcart Prize and for Best of the Net. She is a Professor of English at SUNY / Dutchess Community College in Poughkeepsie, NY.

Lucia Cherciu's web page is
luciacherciu.webs.com.

Printed in the USA
CPSIA information can be obtained
at www.ICGtesting.com
LVHW100200010224
770560LV00003B/359